How You Got to Be You

By Jane Graver

Illustrated by Maritz Communications Company

CONCORDIA

Publishing House
St. Louis

BOOK THREE of the NEW Concordia Sex Education Series

The titles in the series:

BOOK 1: EACH ONE SPECIALLY
BOOK 2: I WONDER WHY
BOOK 3: HOW YOU GOT TO BE YOU
BOOK 4: THE NEW YOU
BOOK 5: LORD OF LIFE, LORD OF ME
BOOK 6: SEXUALITY: GOD'S PRECIOUS GIFT
         TO PARENTS AND CHILDREN

Developed under the auspices of the Family Life Department
Board for Parish Services
The Lutheran Church—Missouri Synod

The Bible text in this publication (marked TEV) is from the Good News Bible, the Bible in TODAY'S ENGLISH VERSION. Copyright © American Bible Society 1966, 1971, 1976. Used by permission.

Copyright © 1982
Concordia Publishing House
3558 South Jefferson Avenue
Saint Louis, Missouri 63118

MANUFACTURED IN THE UNITED STATES OF AMERICA

Library of Congress Cataloging in Publication Data

Graver, Jane, 1931-
    How you got to be you.

    (New Concordia sex education series; book 3)
    Summary: Sex instruction for eight to eleven year olds, with an emphasis on Christian values. Includes male and female physiology, the growth of the fetus, and adolescence.
    1. Sex instruction for children. 2. Sex instruction for children—Religious aspects—Christianity. [1. Sex instruction for children. 2. Sex—Religious aspects—Christianity. 3. Christian life] I. Title. II. Series.
HQ53.G65 1982   241'.66   82-8110
ISBN 0-570-08477-6   AACR2

1 2 3 4 5 6 7 8 9 10   WW   91 90 89 88 82 86 85 84 83 82

Contents

Editor's Foreword

This book is one of a series of six published under the auspices of the Board for Parish Services of The Lutheran Church—Missouri Synod through its Family Life Department.

Other books in the series are: *Each One Specially* (ages 3—5); *I Wonder Why* (ages 6—8); *The New You* (ages 11—14); *Lord of Life, Lord of Me* (ages 14+); and *Sexuality: God's Precious Gift to Parents and Children.*

As the title suggests, the last book is designed for adults, to help them deal with their own sexuality, as well as provide practical assistance for married and single parents in their role as sex educators in the home.

How You Got to Be You is the third book in the series. It is written especially for boys and girls ages 8 to 11—and, of course, for the parents, teachers, and other significant grown-ups who may want to discuss the book with the child. (See the "Note to Parents" at the beginning of this book for suggestions on using the book and ways to communicate Christian values in sex education in the homes.)

Like its predecessor, the new Concordia Sex Education Series provides information about the social-psychological and physiological aspects of human sexuality. But more: It does so from a distinctively Christian point of view, in the context of our relationship to the God who created us and redeemed us in Jesus Christ.

The series presents sex as another good gift from God which is to be used responsibly.

Each book in the series is graded—in vocabulary and in the amount of information it provides. It answers the questions which persons at each age level typically ask.

Because children vary widely in their growth rates and interest levels, parents and other concerned adults will want to preview each book in the series, directing their young person to the next-graded book when he/she is ready for it.

In addition to reading each book, you can use the books as starting points for casual conversation and when answering other questions a young person might have.

This book can also be used as a mini-unit or as part of another course of study in a Christian school setting. (Correlated filmstrips are available for curricular use.) Whenever the book is used in a class setting, it's important to let the parents know beforehand, since they have the prime responsibility for the sex education of their children.

While parents will appreciate the help of the school, they will want to know what is being taught. As Christian home and school work together, Christian values in sex education can be more effectively strengthened.

Frederick J. Hofmeister, M. D., FACOG, Wauwatosa, Wis., served as medical adviser for the series.

Rev. Ronald W. Brusius, Secretary of Family Life Education/Board for Parish Services, served as chief subject matter consultant.

In addition to the staffs of the Board for Parish Services and Concordia Publishing House, the following special consultants helped conceptualize the series: Darlene Armbruster, Betty Brusius, Margaret Gaulke, Priscilla Henkelman, Lee Hovel, Robert Miles, Margaret Noettl, and Rex Spicer.

Earl H. Gaulke

Note to Parents

After you read this book, you may feel quite puzzled. Is all this factual information really necessary for 8- to 11-year olds? It's probably a lot more than we knew when we were that age.

The thing is, our children are living in a different world than the one in which we grew up. They are exposed to distorted information about sex every day—through TV shows, movies, the words to popular music, and from their friends at school (Christian schools too). If they already have a solid foundation of knowledge and attitudes, they can evaluate the shoddy values and the misinformation they get from other sources instead of swallowing them whole.

Research has shown that children are far more likely to develop healthy attitudes about their sexuality when parents encourage discussions about sex. Too much information does not seem to do any harm when linked to positive values. The child who feels unable to ask questions is far more likely to become preoccupied with sex than the one who has open access to information.

Of course, boys and girls from 8 to 11 will vary widely in their ability to understand the material in this book. You are the best judge of what is appropriate for your own children at each stage of their development. To decide whether this book is too advanced or too easy for your child, examine *I Wonder Why* and *The New You*, the books which come before and after the present volume in this series.

How should you use this book? We recommend that you either read it with your child or let him read it and then discuss sections about which he has questions. Most children will not want to read all of it at once. They will probably be interested in different sections at different stages of their development. Another option: Use the book as a "what to say" resource as you talk with your children.

We have a reason for suggesting that sex education begin at an early age. Nearly all the young adults we questioned about their memory of the sex education they had had in their own homes said something like: "Too little, too late. It turned me off to have to listen to a bunch of stuff I already knew—or thought I knew."

Where did these parents go wrong? In many cases they were waiting for questions, ready with carefully planned answers. Sometimes no questions came. Did that mean their children weren't interested? Of course not. Perhaps the children had sensed their parents' discomfort. Or maybe they had learned from others that sex is a subject with a fence around it.

If talking about sex is difficult for you, it might be a good idea to level with your children about your feelings. You could say something like, "This is so special, so private, that it's a little difficult for me to talk about it. But thank you for asking such a good question; that really helps."

You will find that once the ice is broken it will be easier for everyone. Your children will learn better and remember more from a series of conversations than from a long, serious talk that may be put off because of the difficulty of finding the right time and place for it.

Speaking of time and place, be ready for some surprises. When you show your children it's okay to talk about sex, they'll ask questions whenever and wherever they happen to think of them.

Many young people who criticized their parents as sex educators did admit that the parents' attitudes and values did come through, in spite of their clumsiness in expressing them. It's comforting to know that we can make mistakes without necessarily ruining our children, isn't it? Somehow God blesses our bumbling efforts and makes them work far better than we would have dreamed possible.

How to Use This Book

1. You can sit down and read all of the book at once, or you can use the Contents to look up questions you may have. It's a good idea to talk over what you learn with an adult you can trust, like a parent or teacher.
2. Some pages have pictures with labels on them. Be sure to study the pictures and read the labels very carefully.
3. "Some Words Used in This Book" (see p. 58) can help you understand and pronounce the hardest words in this book.
4. When you see this kind of print: *Says who?*—that's what someone your age might say to the writer of this book. The same kind of print is used for the prayers in this book, because they are what someone your age might say to God.

You Are Wonderful!

Says who?

God says so, that's who. He knows you, and He thinks you are terrific.

How do I know He doesn't have me mixed up with some other kid?

God made you different from every other kid in the whole world. In fact, you are different from every other kid who has ever lived! Your fingerprints and your footprints are different from those of any other person. Nobody else has your special mix of hair color, freckles, talents, likes and dislikes, and the million other things that make you you. When God made you, He made one of a kind.

Hey, wait a minute. God made Adam and Eve. But I was born. I came from my mother and father.

That's right. But God was there. Life can come only from God. Your life is a gift from Him, a gift with your name on it.

God knows you. He knows everything about you. And He loves you just as you are (that's not the same as loving everything you do).

You Are Male or Female

Male and female are the words we use to describe a person's **sex**. Your sex is a very important gift from God. If you are a female, it means you can be a mother someday. If you are a male, it means you can be a father. What else does it mean to be male or female?

For instance . . . would you vote for a girl to be president of your class? Would you laugh at a boy who cried when his team lost the game? Should girls be allowed to try out for a school baseball team? Are boys or girls more helpful? more gentle? smarter? braver?

People have changed their thinking quite a bit in the past few years. Although not everyone agrees on the answers to the questions above, we do agree that there are fewer differences between men and women than we used to think. Both men and women have many more choices than they used to have.

Your Feelings Are Important

Not everyone understands that boys and girls have the same feelings. Judy loved to swim, and often raced the other kids at the pool. When Judy was in a race, she put everything she had into winning.

Then someone called Judy a "tomboy." She didn't want to be different from other girls, so she stopped racing. As she lay in the sun with the other girls, Judy told herself she didn't miss racing at all.

But it wasn't true. And she felt so unhappy about giving up swimming that now she had trouble making friends.

Judy needs to listen to her own feelings and not worry so much about what other people say. If she remembers that God loves her just as she is, it will be easier for her to like herself.

Ted's dog Rex was killed by a car. Whenever Ted thought about Rex, he just couldn't help crying—even though he had been told, "Big boys don't cry."

Now Ted felt even worse, because he was afraid people might call him a sissy. He was ashamed to feel sad so long after Rex's death. He told himself, "Rex was a dumb old dog and I don't even miss him." When Ted locked his sad feelings inside himself, his stomach hurt.

Ted should understand that it is normal for a person to cry when he feels sad. (Even Jesus cried. Read about it in John 11:32-35.) People who try to be too tough to cry often become unable to show *any* feelings—love and joy as well as sadness. The bottled up feelings make them unhappy, sometimes even sick.

Ted would probably feel better if he went off by himself and cried when he felt like it. Another time he might say to himself, "Yes, I really feel sad, but if I get busy doing something interesting, maybe my sad feelings will go away." Most of all, Ted needs to remember that he can tell *Jesus* how he feels. Jesus knows how we feel, for He Himself grew up as a human being just like us (except, of course, without sin).

Today's young people are more free to be themselves than their parents were. Some girls like to play soccer or fix bicycles; other girls would rather be cheerleaders or take dancing lessons. Some boys love to draw or play the piano; other boys would rather play football.

Thank God that you have all these choices. God has given you many, many talents. If you try a lot of different activities, you will discover many different things you are good at, things that make you special. And if you have many different interests, you will have many more ways of making friends.

Jesus grew both in body and in wisdom, gaining favor with God and men (Luke 2:52 TEV).

Our High Priest [Jesus] is not one who cannot feel sympathy with our weaknesses. On the contrary, we have a High Priest who was tempted in every way that we are, but did not sin (Hebrews 4:15 TEV).

Jesus went all over Galilee, teaching in the synagogues, preaching the Good News about the Kingdom, and healing people who had all kinds of disease and sickness (Matthew 4:23 TEV).

You were a boy once, Jesus. Like me, You had to learn how to be a man. You chose not to be rough and tough and mean . . . but You were still a real man. You and Your friends hiked from one city to another, helping people. You were brave and independent—and You were also gentle and kind. You loved everyone—and You still do, the Bible says.

Do you really love me, Jesus? Even when I back away instead of trying something hard? When other kids make fun of me, I need to know You think I'm special. Give me the courage to grow to be more like You—and to remember that You love me even when I fail. Be with me, Jesus, as I grow to be a man.

Have you ever felt like the boy in this prayer? Have you ever been teased because you were different from the kids you were with?

That happens to most people at one time or another. Try not to be too worried about what other people say. Talk to Jesus about it. Remember, He loves you no matter what. So just be yourself, the terrific person God made.

God made you a girl or a boy. He will help you grow into a happy woman or man.

Male + Female + God's Gift of Life = BABY

Men and Women: Alike, Yet Different

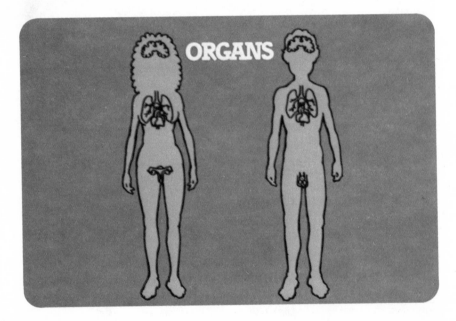

If you could see inside the bodies of a man and a woman, you would find much that is alike. In both men and women the heart pumps blood, the lungs breathe. Many other organs work together to keep the person alive.

Organs?

Body parts like the heart, brain, and lungs are called organs. **Sexual organs** do the work of creating new life. They are different in men and women.

16

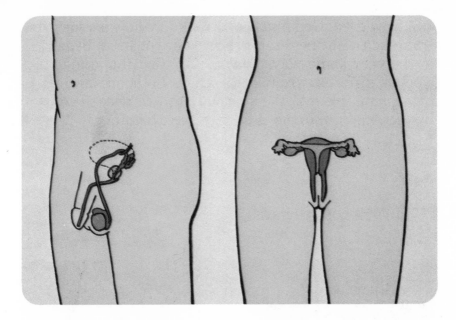

When you began life, you were just one tiny cell, smaller than the dot of an i. This tiny cell that was you was formed when a **sperm cell** from your father joined an **egg cell** from your mother.

Under a strong microscope they'd look about like this.

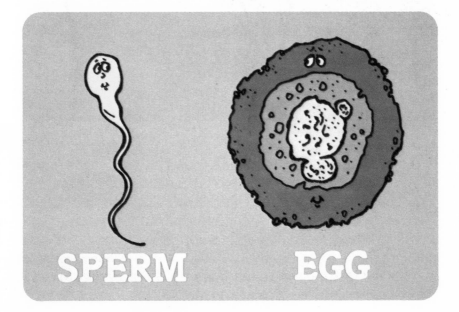

SPERM   EGG

How great God must be, to make a whole person grow from such a tiny beginning! Everyone you know began life in the very same way. That is why God made men and women different from each other. Both are needed to bring new life into the world. Both are needed to love, protect, and guide the child they have begun.

A Man's Sexual Organs

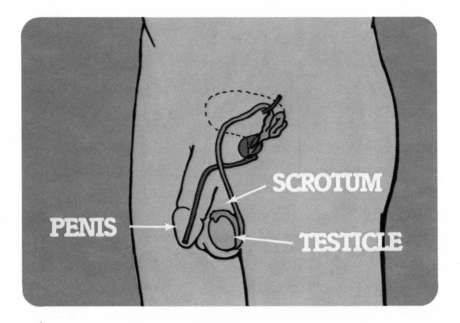

The sperm cell from which you grew was made in one of your father's **testicles**. There are two roundish testicles in a bag of skin called the **scrotum**. The scrotum hangs between a man's legs, just behind and under his **penis**. The penis is a finger-shaped organ which is usually soft and spongy.

In the testicles of a grown man billions of sperm cells grow each month. They are stored in a tube which connects the testicles to the outside of the body through the penis.

When a boy becomes old enough to be a father (approximately between ages 12 and 15), his testicles begin to make sperm cells. His body also makes a milky liquid in which the sperm cells swim. The sperm cells and the milky liquid in which they swim is called **semen.** Semen leaves the body through the penis.

Urine (waste water) also passes from the body through the penis, but never at the same time as semen. The **anus,** where bowel movements leave the body, is behind the testicles.

A Woman's Sexual Organs

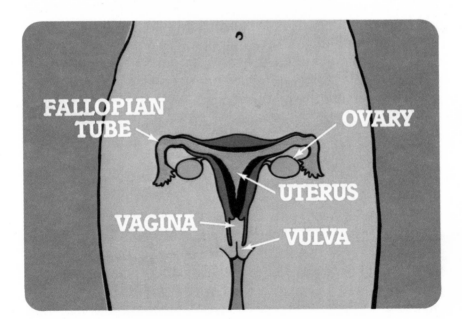

The egg cell from which you grew was made in your mother's **ovary.** A woman has two ovaries deep inside her body, a little lower than her waist. Each one is only as big as an almond; yet thousands of egg cells are stored there.

Between the ages of 10 and 14 (sometimes a little earlier, sometimes a little later) the egg cells in the ovaries begin to change and ripen. After that about once a month an egg cell leaves one or the other ovary.

Near each ovary a hollow tube, called a **fallopian tube**, opens to receive the egg. While passing through this tube, the egg may meet and unite with a sperm and then continue its journey to the **uterus**. If it does not join a sperm, the egg disintegrates.

The uterus lies between the ovaries and just above the bone that forms a bridge between a girl's legs. It is about the size and shape of a pear. This organ can stretch like a balloon to many times its ordinary size. It is here that a fertilized egg cell grows into a baby.

The uterus is connected to the outside of the body by a narrow passageway. This organ, the **vagina**, opens between the legs. It is covered by folds of skin and flesh called the **vulva**. The opening through which urine passes is also within the vulva.

The ovaries, tubes, uterus, vagina, and vulva are the **reproductive** organs of girls and women. All except the vulva are inside the body.

A Brand-new Person

When a sperm cell from your father met and united with an egg cell in one of your mother's fallopian tubes, your life began. In that instant the question of whether you were going to be a boy or girl was decided. There are many sperm cells in a man's semen. About half of them are able to start a girl baby. About half are able to start a boy baby. It all depends on which sperm cell joins the egg cell.

The egg cell and the sperm cell did more than just stick together. In a way only God understands, the two

20

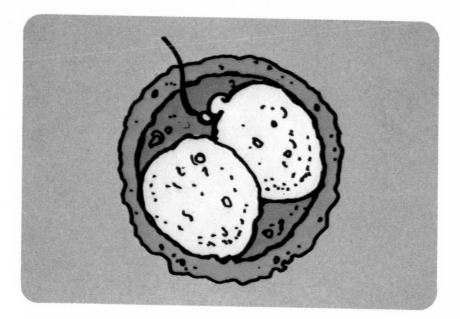

cells changed into one NEW cell—the beginning of a brand-new person!

The speck of new life had in it the color of your hair, the shape of your nose, and the talents that would someday help make you special. That's why you look a little bit like your mother and a little bit like your father.

Then why isn't my hair curly like my dad's? And why are my eyes blue when both my parents have brown eyes?

A woman's body makes hundreds of egg cells in her lifetime. Each of those egg cells has different **genes**, different directions for making a baby. A man makes millions of sperm cells in his lifetime; each one has different genes in it. Your **characteristics**, things like straight hair and blue eyes, were decided by the particular genes in the sperm cell that happened to join the genes in a particular egg cell.

Grandma and I like to go fishing. Did I get "go fishing" genes from her?

Maybe. Your genes might make you more likely to be a person who is good at catching fish. But your experiences—the fun you have with Grandma or the time you caught that big fish—are also important in making you the person you are. Your effort is important, too. You probably try hard to follow Grandma's directions when you fish together.

Your experiences and your hard work will always be an important part of you. You can't change the color of your eyes, but you can become a better reader. You can learn to control your quick temper.

Everyone is born with both strengths and weaknesses. With God's help, you can discover your strengths, your best characteristics, and work to develop them.

You Are an Important Part of a Family

Your family is another of God's gifts to you—and you are God's gift to your family.

Me? God's gift to my family?

That's right. Whether you are the oldest child or a middle one or the youngest, your family would not be complete without you.

Then why do I get blamed for everything?

Very likely your sister or brother would ask the same question. In every family, each child sometimes thinks someone else is the parents' favorite.

The fact is that parents do not treat all their children in the same way. They treat each child a little differently because each child is special. Your parents probably try hard to meet your special needs.

Your family began when your mother and father decided to get married. They wanted to live their lives together. They promised to stick together and take care of each other for as long as they live.

They are "best friends" who trust each other. They ask God to help them be honest with each other. Each knows the other will try to understand.

But sometimes my mom and my dad fight.

How about you? Do you always get along with your best friend?

We-l-l-l . . .

Exactly. We are all sinners—grownups, too. Because Jesus died for us and rose again, we can ask our heavenly Father to forgive us. And we can ask God's Spirit to help us grow as a Christian. We can listen to the other person's side. We can try harder to consider the other person's feelings. We can be more honest about our own feelings.

Even though a husband and wife are best friends, they have to keep working to make their friendship better. In a good marriage they feel so close to each other they are almost like one person.

Not all families have a mother and a father.

Yes. Sometimes sad things happen, like death or divorce. Children in these families often feel that whatever happened must be partly their fault. But there is nothing a child can do to stop such things from happening. There is no way a child can make divorced people want to get married again.

It's important to remember that ALL families have hard times. God is there in good times and in bad. He helps families make the best of things.

No family is perfect. People are never exactly as we would like them to be. But God will help you accept the people in your family as they are. He will help you love and support each other. He will help your love to grow.

Love + Egg + Sperm = God's Plan for New Life

A woman and a man get married because they love each other very much. Each of them has found a special friend, much better than any friend they have ever had. And they *show* their love in many ways. They help each other. They share happy times and sad times. They enjoy

24

just being together. Each married couple has its own favorite ways of showing love for each other.

At times a husband and wife will want to express their love for each other in a special way, called sexual **intercourse.** At those times they will go off by themselves. They will hug and kiss each other and touch each other all over. The husband's penis will become firm and hard, able to fit inside his wife's vagina.

While they are loving each other in this way, semen comes out of the husband's penis. Many sperm cells are in the semen. The sperm cells move up the vagina, through the uterus, and into the fallopian tubes leading to the ovaries. If one sperm cell joins an egg cell in a fallopian tube, new life begins. A baby is started.

A baby does not begin to grow every time a husband and wife have intercourse. An egg cell is in one of the fallopian tubes only a few days each month, and only then can a baby be started.

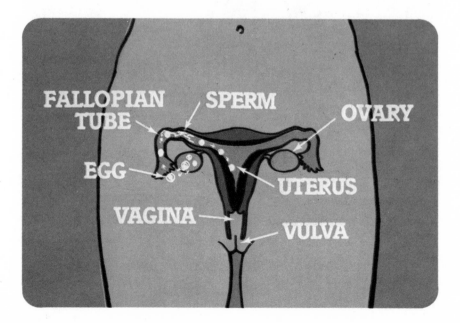

Since it is through intercourse that a baby can begin, God wants only a husband and his wife to make love in this way. Husbands and wives have promised to live together always and to make a home for their children. They as parents will take care of the babies born to them.

Some people decide not to have any children. Some others cannot have children because their sexual organs do not work quite as they should. If you know a couple with no children, don't question them about it. You might hurt their feelings.

Some couples without children want children enough to adopt children whose first parents could not take care of them. They are usually very good parents who love their adopted children very much. God has more than one way of making families!

Friends always show their love. What are brothers for if not to share trouble? (Proverbs 17:17 TEV)

I don't know, God; it sounds pretty strange to me. Why did You invent such a complicated way of starting babies? Sure, I'd like to have a baby of my own someday ... but I can't imagine wanting to be THAT close to anyone ... especially a boy!

I guess maybe it's like asparagus . . . I'll have to wait until I'm grown up to appreciate it. Even now I can see that it would be really nice to have an extra-special friend, someone I could tell anything to and he would understand. Someone who would love me no matter what. Someone who would be there when I needed him.

Thank You for the friends I have now, God. Teach me to BE the kind of friend I'd like to have. Help me get ready for the day when I begin a friendship so special it will last for the rest of my life.

God Took Care of You ...
Right from
the Beginning

Smaller Than a Dot

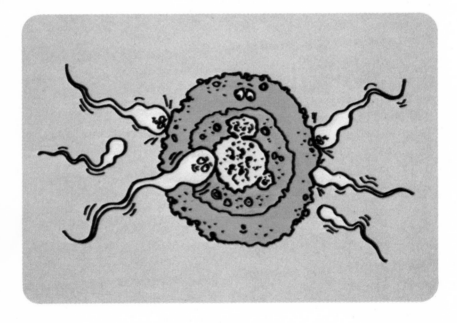

When the egg cell in your mother joined the sperm cell from your father, you were really smaller than the dot on this i.

Soon something wonderful happened. That one new cell that was you divided into two cells. All at once you were twice as big as you had been.

During the next few weeks, you doubled your size again and again. You also moved from the fallopian tube to the uterus, where God had prepared a safe and comfortable place for you to live and grow. (See the drawing on page 25.)

At about two months you were this big. Here is an enlarged picture so you can see what you looked like. Do you see the eyes and ears? Your head was very big compared to your body. You had short arms and legs and fingers and toes. You had the beginnings of a stomach and a brain.

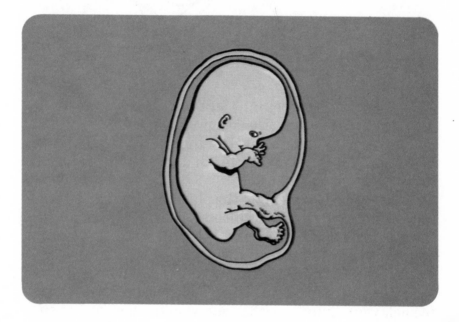

You Were Safe and Warm and Well-Fed

You floated in a bag full of a liquid that was mostly water. It was even more comfortable than the waterbeds some people have. The water acted like a springy cushion, protecting you from bumps. You were always just warm enough. Very hot days or cold days didn't bother you a bit.

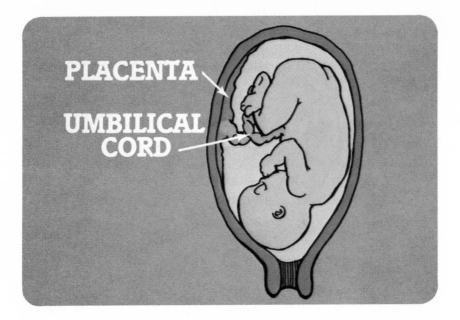

PLACENTA

UMBILICAL CORD

Of course, you couldn't eat and breathe under the water in the same way you do now. Do you see the cord that goes to the baby-to-be's navel (belly button)? The other end of the cord joins the **placenta,** an organ on the wall of the uterus.

Your blood flowed into the placenta. Food and oxygen moved from your mother's blood to yours. Waste materials from your body went into your mother's bloodstream so your mother could get rid of them.

When you had been growing for about four and a half months, you began acting like a newborn baby. You began to suck your thumb, so that you would know how to suck for milk after you were born. Still inside the bag of water, you were big enough to push against the walls of the uterus as you kicked and stretched your arms and legs. For the first time your mother felt a little flutter inside her when you moved. What a thrilling moment that was for her!

Most **pregnant** women have a checkup about once a month to see how the baby is getting along. (The word pregnant means that a woman has a baby growing in her uterus.) In time you were big enough for the doctor to hear your heartbeat with a stethoscope. Most doctors have electronic equipment in their offices which makes it possible for the pregnant mother and the father-to-be and brothers and sisters-to-be to hear the heartbeat of the baby in the uterus.

The Last Few Months Before Birth

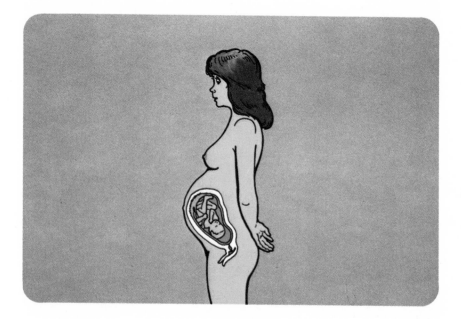

As you grew still bigger, your mother's belly, also known as the abdomen, became big and round. Her uterus stretched to give you more room, but you had to lie more and more tightly curled up. Now your mother knew when you were asleep, because when you were awake you kicked harder against the wall of the uterus.

Although your eyes were still tightly shut, your ears were beginning to work. Loud noises made you jump, and you listened all day to your mother's heartbeat. Sometimes you even had hiccups. The people in your family felt the way you do when you are waiting for Christmas. They could hardly wait for you to be born. They asked all sorts of questions: Will our baby be a boy or a girl? Who will he or she look like? What name shall we choose?

Everyone helped get ready for the big day. Your parents probably fixed a special place for you to sleep. They got baby clothes and diapers and little blankets ready. Your father and sisters and brothers tried to be extra helpful, so your mother could get extra rest. She got tired carrying you around all day!

Your mother packed a little suitcase of clothes for both of you. She wanted to be ready when the time came to go to the hospital where you would be born.

Finally, the Great Day Came

After about nine months you were ready to be born. The uterus began to squeeze and push you out, very gently at first and then with more and more power. Slowly you moved down into the vagina and out through the vulva.

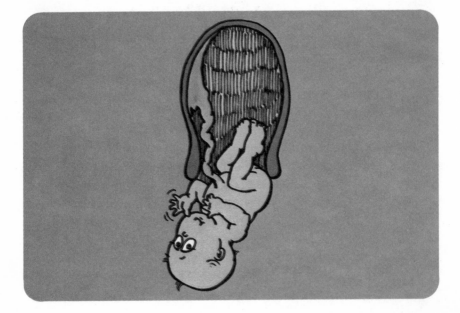

The bag of water broke, and the vagina and vulva stretched to let you come out between your mother's legs.

This was very slow, hard work for your mother. The muscles that squeezed and stretched got very tired, so tired they may have hurt. But your mother probably didn't mind. She was happy and excited because she was about to see you for the first time. The long months of waiting were almost over. Soon she would hold you in her arms.

Although it is possible for a mother to give birth to a healthy baby all by herself, most babies are born in hospitals. The doctor and nurse help make the mother and baby more comfortable. Nowadays the baby's father often helps, too.

The mother and the father want to hold the baby as soon as possible, but first the doctor must make sure that the baby is breathing. Usually the baby begins to cry, and no wonder! The baby is still wet from the bag of water, and the room is much colder than the uterus was.

Once the baby begins breathing it no longer needs the placenta or the cord coming from it. So the doctor cuts the cord. Cutting the cord doesn't hurt the mother or the baby; it's like cutting hair or fingernails.

Soon after the baby is born the mother's uterus pushes out the placenta. The mother's uterus, vagina, and vulva become small again.

Soon the mother's breasts will begin to make milk. In most cases there will be enough milk to feed the baby every day for a long time. When the baby no longer sucks at her breast because he or she drinks from a bottle or a cup, the mother's breasts will stop making milk.

Most babies are not very pretty right after they are born. Often the head has been pushed into an odd shape during birth. The skin is wrinkled and red. After a few days the skin becomes a normal color and the soft bones of the head move back into shape. But the family usually thinks their baby is beautiful, right from the first day!

Human babies are helpless till long after birth. Not only do babies need food, warmth, and cleanliness, but they also need love. A baby that is never held or talked to would probably get sick, and might even die. When babies are older, they still need someone who will love them and help them learn and grow. That's why God's plan for families is so important. Babies and children need people who will love and care for them for many years.

Twins

Once in a while a mother will have two or more babies on the same day. Her uterus has stretched enough to make room for them as they grew. Sometimes the uterus gets too crowded; then these babies are born a little early. Of course, two babies can't come out at the same time, so one is always a few minutes older than the other.

There are two kinds of twins, **fraternal** twins and **identical** twins.

Fraternal twins begin life when two different sperm cells join two different egg cells. Fraternal twins are not much more alike than any other two children in the same family. They might be two boys, two girls, or a boy and a girl.

Identical twins begin life when one sperm cell joins one egg cell. The one new cell splits into two cells, which then grow to become two babies. Identical twins look exactly alike, but they are not. Each one is special. Each has his or her own interests, ideas, personalities, and experiences.

Premature Babies

After nine months in the uterus, babies are ready to live in the world. Some are born after only seven or eight months. These are called **premature** babies. They can grow to be strong and healthy—but they need extra care after they are born. They are usually kept for a while in **incubators**, which keep them warm and away from germs.

Taking Care of Our Bodies

What a great responsibility it is to be pregnant! God entrusts a *whole new life* to the mother. Whatever the mother does affects the unborn baby. That's why it's so important for the mother to take care of her own body especially when she's pregnant.

For instance, doctors have learned that an unborn baby's heart beats much faster after the mother smokes a cigarette. Does this hurt the baby? There is more and more evidence that it does.

You already know that you feel better and look better if you eat right, get enough sleep and exercise, and stay away from drugs that might be harmful. Now you have another reason to take care of your body. If you decide to have a child someday, you will already have formed the good habits that will give your baby a better chance for good health.

When my bones were being formed,
    carefully put together in my mother's womb,*
    when I was growing there in secret,
    You knew that I was there—
    You saw me before I was born
                    (Psalm 139:15-16a TEV).

Lord, You have taken care of me all my life. You have always been right here . . . close to me, loving me, ready to listen. You know me better than I know myself. How wonderful You are!

Do you remember the day I was born, God? I know You were there. I wish I could remember. What did I notice first in this strange new world? What did my family say, I wonder, when they saw me for the first time?

Yes, You remember the day I was born—and the days before that. If You knew me when I was a tiny speck inside my mother, You surely know me now. You know that I love

---

* **Womb** is another word for **uterus.**

picnics and books and climbing trees—and that I hate math and spiders and oatmeal.

You know whether I feel terrific or terrible ... and You care. You can even look into the future and see the grownup person I will be someday.

*I don't understand how You can know me so well, God, and still love me ... but I'm sure glad You do. And I know You love me. Why else did You send Your Son, Jesus, to be **born** in our sinful world? Stay close to me forever.*

My, How You've Grown!

Not really. . . . Lots of people in my class are much taller than I am.

The most important growing happens inside a person. You'll grow on the outside, too, when your body is ready. But I know that you are growing on the inside right now.

What do you mean?

When you were baptized, God made you a member of His family. Now, as you learn about Jesus, you are growing as a Christian.

When you were a little baby, you needed lots of things and you cried and yelled until you got them. Your family gave you food and toys and love. What did you give them? Nothing but a smile.

Now that you are older, you are able to give as well as take. And Jesus helps you. So you do things like setting the dinner table or taking care of younger children when your parents are busy. You notice when they are tired and try to help. You make a special birthday card for someone you love, or just surprise him or her with an extra hug.

Sometimes I don't want to be with my family. I'd rather be alone or with my friends.

That's a part of growing called independence. When you were a baby, you wanted to be with your mother all the time. Even when you began to go to school, it was hard to be away from home so much of the day.

But now you like to stay all night at a friend's house. Maybe you even went somewhere—like camp—by yourself, even though none of your friends were going. Or maybe your family moved, and you went to a new school where you didn't know anyone.

Going alone was hard. It seemed like everyone had a friend to be with, everyone but me. It made me glad to know that Jesus is my Friend!

Did you feel alone for a long time?

It seemed like forever while it was happening. But now that I look back on it, I see that it didn't take long for me to make friends.

Would you go alone again?

It depends. If it's something I really want to do, I'd go alone. Camp, for instance, is so much fun I can put up with the lonesomeness of the first day.

That's another way you have grown up. When you were little, you couldn't wait for things to get better. If little children are asked to choose between ice cream right now and a new bike next month, they pick the ice cream every time.

You know what? I gave up my after-school free time every day for two weeks. I wanted to work on my Science

41

Fair project: The Human Body. It turned out great! It was worth all that time.

Lots of people your age are interested in the human body and how it works. God made your body beautiful and good and interesting . . . all of it.

We-l-l-l, there are SOME parts that aren't so nice. I didn't put sexual organs in my Science Fair model. People would have said it was dirty.

Your sexual organs are private, not dirty. That's why you cover them up, and also why you do not allow anyone else to touch them. Some people have mixed-up ideas about sex, but you know better.

You can feel good about your body because you know God created it. You can thank God for its creation, in words that God's people have used for thousands of years: "I will praise Thee, for I am fearfully and wonderfully made; marvelous are They works!" (Psalm 139:14 KJV).

A Christian will give his body the best of care. He will use it as God wishes him to. He will respect it always.

Some kids sure think sex is dirty. They write words on the bathroom walls, and they tell jokes that make me feel uncomfortable. Half the time I don't get it, but I usually laugh anyway.

As we said, some people do have mixed-up ideas about sex. They might be embarrassed by using the right words for penis and vagina, for instance, so they use slang words instead. Or they get their information from jokes and made-up stories instead of from an adult they can trust, like a parent.

I'd be embarrassed to ask my parents about sex—and I think they'd be embarrassed too.

Maybe. It's a little hard to talk about something that is so private, such a special part of your life. It gets easier, though, the more you do it. And it's smart to talk about important things with people who care enough about you to make sure you get everything straight.

Next Step: Adolescence

A Time of Change

The years when a person changes from a child to an adult are called **adolescence**. Although we think of adolescents as teenagers, some people begin this time of change as early as nine or ten.

Lots of children find it hard to believe that they will ever be interested in the other sex. The idea of changing into a grownup person seems very strange to them. But whether they like the idea or not, those who tell them they will change are right. In a few years boys will probably begin to like girls in a new and special way. When a boy is near a certain girl, he may feel uncomfortable and happy and shy and excited—all at the same time. A girl is likely to have the same feelings when she's with a special boy.

Strong feelings are a part of these growing-up years.

One day you might feel on top of the world; the next day you might feel bitterly unhappy.

You may have strong feelings about people, too. For instance, there may be an older person you admire so much that you walk several blocks out of your way just to pass his or her house.

If you have an adolescent brother or sister, you know that people of this age are often hard to live with. They may burst into tears or slam doors for no reason that anyone else can see. They are so busy growing up they may forget to be patient with younger children in the family.

Adolescents usually want more independence than their parents are ready to give them. It's hard for them to wait until parents are convinced they are responsible enough to handle more freedom.

How Girls Change

When a girl begins to grow up, the shape of her body changes. Her breasts and hips slowly become larger. Hair grows near her sexual organs and under her arms. Within one to three years she might be 6 to 8 inches taller and quite a bit heavier.

About two years after her breasts begin to develop, another important change takes place. An egg cell will move from one of her ovaries to her utuerus. Her body sends extra blood to the uterus, so it will be ready to feed the new life that would begin if that egg cell should join a sperm cell. A soft new lining grows all over the inside of the uterus.

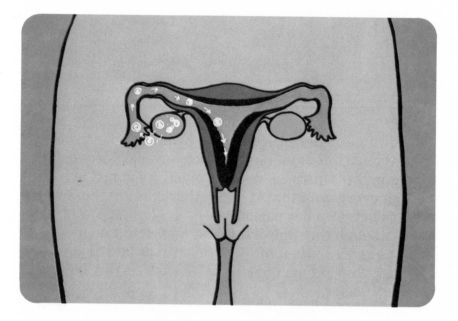

When no baby is started, the egg cell, the new lining, and the extra blood aren't needed. They break up and flow out though the vagina. This is called **menstruation**, and it happens about once a month to nearly every woman.

The unneeded material is mostly blood, and that's what it looks like. Since we think of being hurt when we see blood, menstruation can be scary for a girl who does not understand what is really happening. Remember, this is all *extra* blood that her body does not need, and it comes out very slowly.

Use a calendar to keep track of your periods. Then you will know when to expect the next one.

JANUARY

SUN	MON	TUE	WED	THU	FRI	SAT
1	2	3	④	⑤	⑥	⑦
⑧	⑨	10	11	12	13	14
15	16	17	18	19	20	21
22	23	24	25	26	27	28
29	30	31				

FEBRUARY

SUN	MON	TUE	WED	THU	FRI	SAT
			1	2	③	④
⑤	⑥	⑦	8	9	10	11
12	13	14	15	16	17	18
19	20	21	22	23	24	25
26	27	㉘				

MARCH

SUN	MON	TUE	WED	THU	FRI	SAT
			①	②	③	④
⑤	⑥	7	8	9	10	11
12	13	14	15	16	17	18
19	20	21	22	23	24	25
26	27	28	29	㉚	㉛	

APRIL

SUN	MON	TUE	WED	THU	FRI	SAT
						①
②	3	4	5	6	7	8
9	10	11	12	13	14	15
16	17	18	19	20	21	22
23	24	25	26	27	28	29
30						

A woman's **period** (the time when she is menstruating) lasts about 3 to 7 days. It often takes several years before a young girl's "timer" is regular enough for her to have a period every month. At first there might be several months between her periods.

Although the time of the first menstruation maybe as early as age 9 or 10, it may not be until as late as age 17 or 18. If anything about menstruation worries you, be sure to see your doctor.

After that she will usually menstruate every four weeks until she is 45—50, unless she is pregnant. When a baby is growing in her uterus, the extra blood and the soft new lining are needed for the baby.

What should I do when I start to menstruate?

You will need something to catch the blood, something soft and absorbent. You can wear a **sanitary napkin** or **pad**, which is placed between the legs inside the panties. Some kinds can be fastened right onto the panties; others are fastened to a special belt. Or you can put a **tampon** inside your vagina. A tampon is a small, tight roll of cotton. Discuss with your parents or physician what brand of tampon to use.

Both tampons and sanitary napkins come in different sizes. The smallest size is usually most comfortable for young girls. Packages of 10 or more are sold in drugstores, grocery stores, and discount stores. Instructions come in every package. Ladies' rooms often have coin-operated machines that sell one tampon or one sanitary napkin at a time.

What if I start to menstruate at school?

Most schools keep a supply of sanitary napkins on hand. The school nurse, the school secretary, or a woman teacher are all likely to either have some or know where they are.

But my teacher is a man! What will I tell him?

Tell him the truth. Why not? It's a normal happening, and he knows all about it. If you just can't do that, ask if you can see a woman teacher about a personal problem. He'll understand.

Will anyone be able to tell that I am menstruating?

How could they tell? Of course, it's important to bathe or shower every day. You will soon learn how often you need to change your sanitary napkin or tampon. Most women need a fresh one several times a day, at least during the first day or two. Wrap used napkins in toilet paper and put them in a wastecan, never in a toilet.

When you menstruate, do whatever you usually do. Take gym class, wash your hair, swim (wear a tampon). Some girls have mild pains below their waist, or feel a little tired and crabby during the first day or two. These girls might choose to cut down on very active sports, but they will probably find that some exercise makes them feel better.

If you are a girl, you can look forward to the day you begin to menstruate. It's a sign that you are on your way to becoming a woman. Of course, you still have a lot further to go. Your body may be ready for motherhood, but your mind and spirit still have a great deal of growing to do.

How Boys Change

Boys usually have their time of fast growth a couple years later than girls do. A boy may grow very fast for a year or two, then continue to grow more slowly until he is 20 or so.

When a boy begins to grow taller and heavier, other changes take place in his body. Hair grows around his penis and under his arms. His testicles get bigger because they are beginning to make sperm cells.

Most adolescent boys are more comfortable if they wear an **athletic supporter** when they participate in active sports. The athletic supporter (or jockstrap) is a kind of underpants. It's elastic. It holds the testicles and penis close to the body, where these sensitive organs are less likely to be hurt.

As time goes on, the boy will notice hair beginning to grow on his upper lip. His voice gradually becomes deeper. His testicles continue to grow, and his penis becomes bigger. His shoulders are broader and his muscles more powerful. More hair appears on his chin; soon he will be ready to shave for the first time.

An adolescent boy will have an **erection** more often than he did when he was little. His penis becomes **erect**—that is, instead of being limp and soft, it becomes hard and stands out from his body.

Often there is no reason for the erection. It just happens. In a few minutes the penis goes back to its usual size. As the boy grows older, he will have more control over his penis.

When a boy is somewhere between 12 and 15, he is old enough to have **ejaculations**—semen shooting out from his penis. Often this happens when he is asleep. We call it a "wet dream" because the boy may have a strange and exciting dream about a girl at the same time.

There is no reason to feel guilty or embarrassed about any part of a wet dream. Wet dreams are normal. Wipe off the sperm with some tissue—but don't worry about it. Parents know that adolescent boys have wet dreams.

If you are a boy, when you have your first ejaculation you will know you have taken an important step toward becoming a man. Of course, it is only a first step. Although your body is ready for fatherhood, your mind and spirit still have a lot of growing to do.

Am I Normal?

Nearly everyone asks this question while they are growing up. Twelve-year-old Steve feels like a freak because his eleven-year-old sister Beth is taller than he is. Beth doesn't like it either. She feels like a giant because she is taller than any of her friends. She doesn't like being the only girl in her class who wears a bra.

Both Steve and Beth should try hard to be patient. In a few years Steve might be tall enough to be a basketball star, and Beth might be no taller than she is now. They are both normal, and have been all along.

Different Rates of Growth

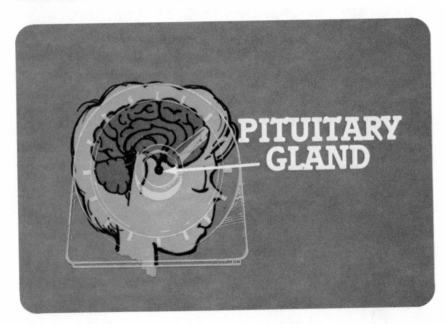

Beth and Steve might feel better if they knew that everyone's growth is controlled by a tiny organ called the

pituitary gland. The pituitary gland is something like an automatic timer. It sends chemicals called **hormones** into the body. One hormone controls the way bones grow. Another controls changes in a person's sexual organs.

Each person's timer is set a little differently. You might begin the changes of adolescence anytime from 9 until 14. In fact, there are some cases of people who begin even earlier or even later. The average girl will do her growing about two years before the average boy. There is so much variety among normal children, though, that a boy might enter adolescence before his twin sister.

Most people would rather do this extra growing at exactly the same time as their friends. Both early growers and late growers sometimes feel out of things during the time they are different from their friends. If this happens to you, try to be content with your own rate of growth. It is right for you.

Try to guess the age of each of these girls and each of these boys. Then look on page 52 to see if you were right.

Temporary Problems

Some of these boys and girls look very different than they did a year or two ago. It might be a little hard for them to get used to being so much taller and heavier than they were. Since hands and feet grow first, young people often feel awkward and out of proportion. Muscles don't usually develop as fast as bones do, so they end up trying to make an adult-size body work with child-size muscles. Hard though it is, the best thing they can do is laugh at their own problems, remembering that the problems won't last long.

Many boys and girls worry about the weight they gain at this age. Others have the opposite problem. They get tall so fast they don't grow sideways at all! Both the chubby look and the skinny look will go away in time IF they exercise and eat the right foods.

Circumcision

If you are a boy, you might have noticed something else that makes you different from some other boys. Some boys were **circumcised** when they were very young. A doctor cut off the foreskin, a loose fold of skin covering the end of the penis.

In Bible times God's people had their boy babies circumcised. This was a sign that they belonged to God's special people. Joseph and Mary took Jesus to be circumcised when He was eight days old. Even today most Jewish parents continue this custom. So do many parents who are not Jewish. They believe that circumcision aids

Answer to "Try to Guess These Ages" (Page 51)
The girls are all 12 years old. The boys are all 14. All of these young people are normal.

good health. It is easier to keep the penis clean when the foreskin is gone.

Different Shapes and Sizes

Adolescent girls often worry about the size and shape of their breasts; boys often worry about the size and shape of testicles and penises. "Am I normal?" they wonder.

Normal people come in many different shapes and sizes. Even in the same person, one breast (or one testicle) may be bigger than the other.

Think how uninteresting life would be if everyone looked exactly alike! Instead, God has made each one of us special in some way. Each of us has some kind of handicap, too—something we don't like about ourselves.

You have a choice. You can spend your life crying about something you cannot change. Or you can make the most of the good gifts God has given you.

Jesus grew both in body and in wisdom, gaining favor with God and men (Luke 2:52 TEV).

Jesus, did You ever worry about growing up? I want to be older, to be powerful and adventurous and independent— but I'm afraid. Now that I see my body beginning to change, half of me would like to keep on being a child.

What will my life be like when I grow up? How will I ever make the right choices? What if I make a mistake?

Put Your hand on my shoulder, Jesus, when I feel panicky about the future. Remind me that You were my age once and that You understand how I feel.

Remind me that one part of my future is sure: You will be there. If I make a mistake, You will forgive me and help me learn from it. You have promised to be with the people who love You. Right now, You are closer to me than I can imagine.

With Your help I can respect and care for the wonderful body You have given me. I can use Your power as I think and speak and grow and love.

It's Great to Be Alive!

When God finished making the world, He looked it all over and saw that it was good. He had made many, many different kinds of plants and animals. Each one was valuable in its own way.

God made each living thing able to bring new life into the world. Each is able to reproduce itself—to make more of its own kind.

Some flowers, for instance, reproduce when bees bring pollen (yellow powder) from one flower to another. The pollen is like sperm cells. Seeds are formed when pollen joins the egg cells in the center of a flower.

A female fish lays many eggs in the water. The male

fish swims over them and sprinkles them with sperm cells. New life begins wherever an egg and a sperm join.

Other animals reproduce themselves very much as humans do. For instance, male dogs, elephants, and mice all have a penis which they use to place sperm inside the female body.

But animals cannot love their mates in the way that humans do. They cannot have the same respect and care for each other. They can never have the joy humans find in a "best friends" marriage.

Animals often take very good care of their babies . . . for a while. Mother elephants take care of their babies for four years, much longer than most other animal mothers. But human babies need much more care, love, and teaching than any animal. They need parents who are able to make wise decisions, parents who can give them a good home for many years.

It takes a long time to grow up enough to be a good parent. Even for an adult, it's not an easy job. All parents make mistakes—sometimes serious ones.

It's a good thing that God has special love for the people He made. What would we do if Jesus had not lived and died for us? Christian parents and children know that God forgives their mistakes for Jesus' sake. They know that God can and will help when trouble comes.

If you have children of your own someday, you will find great joy in loving and caring for them. You will have used God's good gift of sex to bring very special persons into the world. By your love and care you can show your children a little of what God's love is like.

God's love can make your sex a wonderful part of your love for another person. Guided by Him, you can choose a husband or wife who will share your life. The love you have for each other will be extra-special if God lives in both of you.

That time seems a long way in the future, doesn't it? The growing years ahead of you are also God's gift—your time to get ready for adult life. You will learn to make good decisions, remembering that you are God's person. You can stay in touch with Jesus by reading and hearing about Him—and talking to Him in prayer. That way you can grow closer to Him every day. You can discover good ways to use all the wonderful gifts He has given you.

Following God's will always, you'll be able to say, "It's good to be alive!"

SOME WORDS USED IN THIS BOOK

adolescence (a-doh-LES-sense) The years when a person changes from a child to an adult.

athletic supporter (ath-LET-ik suh-PORT-er) A kind of elastic underpants which hold the testicles and penis close to the body.

anus (AY-nuss) The opening from which bowel movements leave the body.

characteristics (kar-ik-tuh-RISS-tiks) The traits or qualities that make a person or thing special. A good singing voice, long legs, and brown eyes are all characteristics a person might have.

circumcision (sur-kum-SIZH-un) A minor operation in which the loose skin, or foreskin, is removed from the end of the penis.

ejaculation (ee-jack-yoo-LAY-shun) A discharge (coming out) of semen from the penis.

erection (ee-RECK-shun) A time when the penis is stiff and stands out from the body.

fallopian tube (fal-LOW-pee-an) The tube inside a woman's body which provides a passage for the egg cell from the ovary to the uterus.

fraternal twins (fruh-TUR-n'l twins) Twins who grew from two different egg cells which were joined by two different sperm cells.

gene (JEEN) A tiny part of a sperm cell or egg cell which carries characteristics from the father or the mother.

hormones (HOR-mones) Chemicals that control growth or other changes in the body.

identical twins (eye-DEN-ti-k'l twins) Twins who grew from one egg cell which divided in two after it was joined by one sperm cell.

incubator (IN-kyoo-bay-ter) A usually glassed-in bed, specially equipped for babies who were born too soon.

intercourse (IN-ter-kors) The act in which sperm cells leave a man's body and enter a woman's body.

jockstrap (JOCK-strap) An athletic supporter, elastic underpants which hold the penis and testicles close to the body.

menstruation (men-stroo-AY-shun) The monthly flow through the vagina of unneeded blood and tissue from the uterus.

organ (OR-gun) A part of the body that has a particular job to do.

ovary (OH-vuh-ree) The female organ in which egg cells develop and grow.

penis (PEE-niss) The male organ through which both urine and semen leave the body.

period (PEER-ee-ud) The regular monthly time during which a woman menstruates, usually 3 to 7 days.

pituitary (pih-TYOO-ih-ter-ee) The tiny group of cells (gland) that makes hormones controlling body growth and the work of many organs in the body.

placenta (pluh-SEN-tuh) A special organ that develops on the wall of the uterus during pregnancy. The placenta helps food and oxygen move from the mother's bloodstream to the baby's bloodstream, and carries wastes from the baby to the mother.

pregnant (PREG-n'nt) Carrying a growing baby in the uterus.

premature (pree-muh-TYOOR) Born too early, before the usual nine months of growing in the uterus has passed.

reproduce (ree-proh-DOOS) To make more of the same kind.

sanitary napkin (SAN-ih-ter-ee NAP-kin) A soft pad used to catch the unneeded blood, etc., that flows from a woman's uterus during menstruation.

scrotum (SKROH-t'm) The bag of skin in which the testicles hang between the legs of a male.

semen (SEE-m'n) A milky liquid that has sperm cells in it.

sexual organs (SEKS-shoo-ul) The body organs needed for reproduction, the creation of new life.

tampon (TAM-pahn) An absorbent plug placed in the vagina to catch the unneeded blood, etc., that flows from a woman's uterus during menstruation.

testicle (TESS-ti-k'l) The male organ in which sperm cells grow.

uterus (YOO-ter-us) The female organ inside which a baby grows.

vagina (vuh-JY-nuh) A tunnel leading from the uterus to the outside of the body.

vulva (VUL-vuh) The lips or folds of skin and flesh that protect the opening to the vagina.

wet dream (WET DREEM) A dream during which semen comes out of the penis.

womb (WOOM) Uterus, the female organ inside which a baby grows.

Date Due

SEP. 25 1988			